AF093585

# FACING (IN)JUSTICE IN HEALTH

BALTIMORE, MARYLAND

STÉPHIE-ANNE CASSAGNOL
DULIÈPRE, LAUREN BRERETON COX,
ANGÉLIQUE BLACK MCKOY, RAMA
IMAD, KRISTIN TOPEL, MINDI B. LEVIN

THE FACING PROJECT PRESS

THE FACING PROJECT PRESS

An imprint of The Facing Project
Muncie, Indiana 47305
facingproject.com

First published in the United States of America by The Facing Project Press, an imprint of The Facing Project and division of The Facing Project Gives Inc., 2025.

Copyright © 2025. All Rights Reserved.

No part of this book may be reproduced, stored in a retrieval system, transmitted in any form by any means (electronic, mechanical, photocopying, recording, scanning, or otherwise) or used in any manner without written permission of the Publisher (except for the use of quotations in a book review). Requests to the Publisher for permission should be sent via email to: howdy@facingproject.com. Please include "Permission" in the subject line.

First paperback edition May 2025

*Cover design by Shantanu Suman*

Library of Congress Control Number: 2025939476

ISBN: 979-8-9902900-3-7 (paperback)
ISBN: 979-8-9902900-4-4 (eBook)

Printed in the United States of America
10 9 8 7 6 5 4 3 2 1

# Contents

| | |
|---|---|
| Foreword | V |
| SECTION I: Breaking Cycles<br>From Surviving to Thriving | 1 |
| 1. From Subjects to Partners: Rewriting the Narrative of Health Research in Baltimore | 2 |
| 2. The Brownstone | 6 |
| 3. To My 10-Year-Old Self | 9 |
| 4. Norwood's Story – It's Common but Not Commonly Heard: Being a Tough Man in Soul and Spirit | 14 |
| 5. Glowing on the Inside and Out | 18 |
| 6. Locked In a Nightmare Cage | 21 |
| 7. A Letter to My Patients | 25 |
| SECTION II: Building Trust | 28 |
| 8. Life-ing It in Community | 29 |
| 9. Where Generations Meet: My Story with Lori's Hands | 32 |
| 10. The Line | 34 |
| 11. The Missing Pillar of Public Health | 37 |

| | |
|---|---|
| SECTION III: Agent of Change | 40 |
| 12. Routine/Rutina | 41 |
| 13. Giving Back: Public Service Worker, Advocate, and Community Member | 45 |
| 14. Navigating Injustice in Healthcare: A Narrative of Hope | 48 |
| 15. Syringes and Stigma | 51 |
| 16. Chasing Shadows | 53 |
| Discussion Reflection Questions | 56 |
| Acknowledgements | 61 |
| Sponsors | 65 |
| About SOURCE | 66 |
| About Transform Mid-Atlantic | 67 |
| About Glick Philanthropies | 68 |
| About The Facing Project | 69 |

# FOREWORD

It is an honor to introduce *Facing (In)Justice In Health*, a remarkable collaboration featuring the voices of 16 talented storytellers, each bringing their unique expertise and insights to the table. Each storyteller was matched with a writer who brought their story to life. In a world that often celebrates the individual, this book stands as a testament to the power of collaboration and the richness that emerges when diverse perspectives converge.

Each story has its own distinct voice, weaving together a tapestry of ideas that explores the major themes: breaking cycles: from surviving to thriving, building trust within communities, and being an agent of change. The combined expertise and life experiences shared in these stories not only deepens our understanding but also invites us to rethink how to navigate the difficult situations that life sometimes throws at us.

Part one begins with Donald's story navigating the impacts of institutional research on Baltimore's Black communities and working to disrupt and overcome this legacy. E. W. Young's story shows us the clear linkages between reliable housing, health and safety, while Monica invites us to explore what it means to challenge others' expectations of us while searching for community in a new country and city. Norwood's story explores what it means to push back on society's narrow definition of masculinity while overcoming threats in our own homes. Tevis shows how the often-invisible mental health battles only exacerbate other challenges in our lives and how impactful it can be to find others who understand these unique struggles. Terry's story, on the other hand, shows vividly what it can mean to be in the crosshairs of a loved one's mental health battles and how quickly we need to prioritize our safety as a result. Dr. Balmuri closes out part one by crafting a heartfelt letter to validate their patients' worries and fears and committing to help disrupt a system that only furthers health disparities.

Part two explores what it means to repair trust in the community, beginning with Carol's moving account of their journey to community health work and the impact of community members like Bea Gaddy who worked tirelessly to uplift her community even at her own expense. Michelle explores her own role in healing the community around her as a nursing student while Angela shares with us what it is like to dedicate oneself to being a refuge to a community in need of the most basic necessities. Finally, David's story weaves for us a journey of self-discovery and how the power of storytelling can help to bridge the schism between the local community and academic institutions.

In part three, Karen begins by sharing how one can make the difference in communities impacted by language barriers and being undocumented. Tynicha highlights how her mother planted the seed of change in her and inspired a lifetime of community work and advocacy. In Adam's story, we see how the impact we have on others comes in many ways such as being a listening ear and ensuring that others feel heard even if we don't hold all the answers. Isabel shows us that one's personal tragedies such as substance abuse and the stigma associated with this, can help fuel a drive to change the world around us for the better. The book ends with a powerful account by Sequean as he guides us through his life experiences with foster care, sense of self, and all the barriers posed by the healthcare system and how this fuels him to advocate for a brighter future for the next generation.

As we have had the privilege of witnessing this collaboration unfold, we can attest to the dedication and passion each storyteller and writer has poured into their contributions. We recognize and do not take lightly the immense privilege that is our storytellers sharing such intimate pieces of their lives with us. For that, we are grateful, and we thank each of our storytellers with the assistance of their writers, for the hard and intentional work they put into every word, for their vulnerability and their strength in sharing this powerful gift with all of us.

The discussions, debates, and shared insights that shaped this book have resulted in a work that is both thought-provoking and essential for anyone interested in health equity in Baltimore. We invite you to dive into the pages of *Facing (In)Justice In Health* and engage with the diverse perspectives offered by these storytellers. Their collective wisdom promises to inspire, challenge, and expand your horizons.

As you embark on this journey through *Facing (In)Justice In Health*, we urge you to keep an open heart and mind. Let the stories and perspectives ignite a passion for you to become an agent of change, go from surviving to thriving, and build trust within your own communities. This book is not just a collection of ideas; it is a call to action. Embrace the lessons within these pages and allow them to inspire you to make a difference in your own life and community.

**Content warning:** Please be aware that due to the personal nature of the stories that there will be references to violence, trauma, poverty, addiction, drug use, racism, inequality, loss and medical procedures.

Lauren Brereton Cox
Stéphie-Anne Cassagnol Dulièpre
on behalf of the Facing (In)Justice in Health Steering Committee

# SECTION I: BREAKING CYCLES FROM SURVIVING TO THRIVING

# FROM SUBJECTS TO PARTNERS: REWRITING THE NARRATIVE OF HEALTH RESEARCH IN BALTIMORE

## DONALD YOUNG'S STORY AS TOLD TO MICHELLE MOFFA

Growing up in Park Heights, zip code 21215, health research was taboo. In the collective memory of Baltimore's Black community, "research" brought up the evils of Tuskegee and the injustices of Henrietta Lacks. To even consider participating was unthinkable. We walked down Monument Street and heard primates screeching from the top of Johns Hopkins. *You want to be a guinea pig like that? Don't you remember Uncle Ricky? He used to go to Johns Hopkins every week until one day he never came back. Seventeen years we haven't seen Uncle Ricky.* I knew there were clinical trials, experiments done on animals and humans to develop medications. But in my mind, Black people were not involved. Research was a horror of the past. Research was something done _to_ my community, not for us and certainly not with us.

Today, I walk around Northeast Market two Wednesdays a month, proud to see a new story about health research being written in my community. The smells of fresh fried steak fish and Szechuan flavors float above the tables of Johns Hopkins employees offering free blood pressure measurements and plastic props explaining prostate exams. Across from colorful produce vendors, sits a student typing honest notes about who the Baltimore community is and what we need. I see health inequities laid bare here—I see gunshot wounds and mental health struggles, food deprivation, and chronic diseases. But I also see hope. Projects are coming down from the ivory tower of Johns Hopkins to shrink the health inequity gap just a little. I am filled with awe and gratitude to be in this space where these two worlds collide.

My journey to my position as a community health worker (CHW) was not short or straightforward. There was a time in my life when I did not think I would live to see age 25. I finished my military service and found myself in a life of self-sabotage and heroin addiction. Recovery turned into relapse after I lost my mother to a fentanyl overdose in 2016. A positive HIV test the next year was followed by an overdose on December 17, 2017. I heard the voice of God call my name that day. I got clean, and looked for something to give my life meaning.

I started out at the Baltimore City Health Department, which saw value in my lived experiences and my intersectional identity. Knowing so many different communities—the African American community, the LGBTQIA community, the substance use community—made me the ideal person to carry out a city needs assessment. Various projects and positions later, I was hired by Johns Hopkins to bridge the divide between my community and the academic healthcare and research spheres. My job is not about medical expertise or clinical skills; I don't need a stethoscope to know the heartbeat of my community. I know its pain points intimately because I've lived them. I feel the injustice of Henrietta Lacks, but I also know that my life-saving HIV medications and the medication that my little nephew takes for sickle cell anemia are because of those HeLa cells. I can tell my community that the type of research done in the past is not the research of today. I may not know what happened to Uncle Ricky, but I know that people who consent to be part of a research trial in 2024 will be informed and safe. Folks like me are in the room and at the table now.

However, community health research alone does not close the equity gap. A $10 or $20 gift card two months later for answering a survey—full of the same questions and Likert Scales our community members have been hearing over and over since they were toddlers sitting on their grandmothers' laps—does not show that anyone really cares. No dollar amount can truly compensate for the cost of sharing sensitive, personal details about yourself or being reminded year after year that you are stuck in the bottom income tier listed on the demographics questionnaire. It seems like the academics always get what they came for: they climb the academic ladder, bring in more grant money, publish findings in a journal article that might as well be written in a different language. But what does the community receive?

The community has a right to knowledge. Researchers need to go back to the community and tell them in plain words what the data showed. More importantly, we need to tell them what we're going to do about it. We can't settle for dropping a note in my elderly neighbor's mailbox saying she might be exposed to lead in her home. No, we need to send someone down into her basement to check her pipes and take a water sample. *Develop. Implement. Listen. Teach.* Those are the words that really matter to us.

The community has a right to transparency. And not just symbolic transparency where the university buildings have glass walls so everyone can see inside. How is the data being used and how is the money being spent? We need real honesty and authenticity in community relationships where everyone walks away from the table feeling like the partnership is a win-win, rather than feeling like they got one over on us.

The community has a right to certainty. We see a car dealership worth of luxury vehicles in the Johns Hopkins parking lots, while community health programs and even my job as a community health worker (CHW) are all subject to the whims of a grant. Research shows CHW's generate $3 per dollar invested, yet I can't assure the community members I represent that I will still have a job after July 31st. It feels as though at any second the funding can dry up, the research methodology could change, and the rug could be pulled out from under me and from under my community. My imposter syndrome tells me that a recovering addict from Park Heights does not deserve to be in my position. But the genuine words of appreciation from members of my community reminds me that not only do I deserve to be here, but both the community and the institution *need* me to be here.

When confronting these continued challenges, I choose to see the glass half-full. I see the shortcomings of past and present health research, but I am also confident that we are moving in the right direction. We are elevating voices that were previously silenced or marginalized and we will use the knowledge we gain to make real changes in tackling health inequities together. My own journey—from the dark place of addiction to now walking around Northeast Market as a community leader and advocate—shows that transformation is possible, not just for individuals but for entire communities. I am committed to shaping a future where research is not something done _to_ us, but rather done in a collaborative spirit _with_ us. I know we're just a step away.

# The Brownstone

## E. W. Young's Story as Told to Celine Arar

The brownstone was 1500 square feet for $800 a month. It was a steal—a blessing. The day we moved in, my children and I carried boxes past the small front yard with patchy daffodils and overgrown weeds. We walked across the bright red porch and through the front door. Finally, we were home.

I used to collect varsity collegiate jackets. I loved their colorful and cracked leather and the stories they told through their wear. But my husband had covered so many of them in my blood that I couldn't look at them and I don't wear collegiate jackets anymore. My children and I left as soon as we could. First, we went to Florida. But I always wanted to come back home to Baltimore and I was excited when I found this brownstone. Someplace affordable, someplace our own. It seemed almost impossible that something so solid could hold so much meaning.

My relief didn't last very long.

A couple of weeks into our rental, our upstairs neighbor fell through the stairs. It was a freak accident I had thought. A freak accident I had told my children when they asked. When my landlord repaired the steps, I noticed he did so with the same wood, nails, and equipment that had been there previously. But when would the next step break? Whose foot would be broken when it did?

A few weeks later, I was lying in bed, breastfeeding my son and counting his ticklish toes. I heard a pitter patter and looked through the gap in my door to rats playing tag on our couch. I remember feeling shocked by their audacity. What else was living behind our walls? What conditions did this create for my children too small to fend anything off themselves?

A month or so after that, I had just stepped into the shower when I noticed round clumps of black in the shower. They looked like the heads of dark dandelions. I called the city and asked them to send someone. When he arrived, he noted that the mold in our building was 50,000x the acceptable level. Was this what had caused my perpetual cold? The cancer I would be diagnosed with a year after leaving?

The next time, when the basement unit door couldn't close correctly, I told the landlord these conditions were unsafe—that we deserved to live in an apartment with a door that closed fully and correctly, with usable facilities, and a strong foundation. He gestured broadly at my neighbors and the homes down our street. Look at the neighborhood you live in, he said with impatience. Look where you are. I glanced around me. Didn't we all deserve high living standards? Didn't we all deserve habitable conditions regardless of our zip code?

After that, I stopped asking questions that went unanswered. I took my children and we moved in with the husband I had gone to Florida to escape. Finding my own apartment in Baltimore, a moment that should have been one of independence and pride, was taken from me. Instead, it became a time of unwilling dependence.

My children and I spent as little time indoors while living there. But it was untenable and we moved into a shelter instead. I worked at a cleaning company during the day and would pick up my children after school. We made up games for one another and spent hours outdoors, watching sunsets from parks and sidewalks. I must have known all the playgrounds in Baltimore. Those slides and swings and monkey bars became our saving grace.

People have said I'm strong, but I don't think that's the right word. I like the word resilient better. I know how it feels to have part of my independence taken from me and I've seen how unresolved trauma begets more trauma. I overcame what felt like insurmountable obstacles to be in the position I'm in now, where I use my experiences to support others. Today, I advocate for domestic violence awareness and welfare benefits for those in need. My feet echo as I walk across the tiled floors and everyone at city hall knows my name.

For my family, I've built a wall around myself and my children that my ex-husband can't break down. For my community, I work to end the cycle of violence that so many are caught in and keep another mother from having to make an impossible choice.

# To My 10-Year-Old Self

## Monica Guerrero Vazquez's Story as Told to Maisie Conrad

I.

It's early morning when I reach the venue, my car packed to the brim with supplies for the conference. I'm a functionally anxious person, and even though I have everything planned and checklists, my mind races with all the day's tasks: *will there be enough food later, did I send the right address?* But there's something else beneath the buzzing thoughts. This weekend, my mother sent me a picture of my grandma for Mother's Day. It's been years since I've seen her, and although that's just life as an immigrant, it's hard to stay present when I'm always thinking ahead to when I can be with my family. Not only will this conference commemorate a decade of Centro SOL—it also marks the 10th year I've been with the organization. I've been reflecting on my work, and all its ups and downs. As I start to unload boxes, another thought comes: *am I doing the right thing?*

It's been a winding path to get where I am now. I come from a humble family in rural Ecuador. My parents grew up very poor, and almost nobody in my family went to college let alone to graduate school; still, my parents supported and encouraged me to study. College, to me, was a way to empowerment. I had seen domestic violence in my family growing up, and when my sister and I would imagine ourselves as adults, we had a car, wore suits (like Madonna), and said *we will never get married!* Not because we were so independent, but because we were so scared of men. With college, I could come back to Ecuador to help my community. I would open schools and grow food in rural communities among the fields and nature; I had grown up in Madrid, a city with nothing but buildings.

My school teachers used to repeat that girls like me don't go to college. My counselor in high school told me I should go to college for medicine because I had good grades in the science track. But medicine was long—eight or nine years and I wanted to finish school quickly so that my parents could stop working all day, every day. Then my counselor suggested computer science, saying *it's going to be the future.* So I did.

II.

At the Centro SOL's conference, people have started to arrive. A state delegate traveled here to present, and she greets me like we knew each other well—so flattering! Many of our community health workers came early to the event just to show their support. These moments of connection are one of the things I love about my work.

When I was in college, I was awarded a scholarship to go back to Ecuador as an expert on mission. The United Nations had me doing IT in a remote rural area of the Andes. The computers had poor signal—the work didn't feel useful. But then, I had the opportunity to spend a lot of time working with kids in the local schools. All the children in that town had at least one parent who had migrated—it was a huge crisis. There was depression, stigma, and substance use problems. But I didn't have that terminology back then, I just felt something was off the whole time.

I returned to Spain, and decided that if I wanted to make a change in the lives of those children, I had to learn more, so I finished grad school. This connected me with international cooperation. But as I was planning a project in rural Andes in Bolivia to work with women, life happened and I moved to the US. I wanted to meet more Latinos. I didn't feel very connected with my identity in Spain; my accent, my look, it all screamed out that I wasn't from there. The discrimination was awful. In the US I found myself in a more diverse community—I could see people who look like me. I used to want thin, brownish hair that looks blonde when the sun hits it. I eventually came to love how black, thick and heavy mine is. This is my identity, my roots are Indigenous, and I love it.

I came to Baltimore, and after a period of being uninsured, and unemployed in a new country, I eventually started work for Centro SOL. There, I dug deeper into the things I saw in Ecuador; now I knew the abuse was intimate partner violence, the depression was very stigmatized. I thought, engineers are nice people, but they don't know about these subjects like those in public health do (smile). I also learned how important it is for me to be recognized as an Ecuadorian. If you say to someone in the community *I'm Latina*, people don't really care. But if you say *I'm Ecuadorian*, you'll have people say *Oh, I'm Ecuadorian, too!* Or *I have a friend from Ecuador*. Many people in the US are categorized as Latino, but they come from a vast array of diverse communities, and they all deserve recognition and respect.

III.

Food is sacrosanct to me, so at each event I always provide a meal from local Latino artisans. At today's conference we got to enjoy a wonderful spread of Mexican cuisine. The table is covered with tacos, taquitos, tortillas, and hard boiled eggs. And rice, lots of rice. I look around the table of people eating and talking together as one. When I started community work, we'd often say *we're going to help them.* Now I say, *No, we don't do that*. We partner, we collaborate, we reach out—we don't help. I am inspired by the diversity of Baltimore's Latino community, and want to step away from the egocentric ways we approach it.

There were six workers, Latinos, who were working on the Key Bridge when it collapsed. Some of their families reached out to me to get connected to resources. I asked them if they had immigration status, and I learned that most of them were US born. But all the news and social media, everybody talked about them as if they were undocumented. The problem is that if we say undocumented all the time when we're trying to describe a population, we get stuck. This is not a synonym for Latinos. One of the families preferred help from the Mexican embassy to access a therapist, even though their insurance would cover more. To me, this showed failure to build pathways for Latinos of all immigrant statuses to access services they have rights to.

We can do a better job of speaking positively about the Latino community. They are marginalized, they are not "the needy." We train Latinos to be ambassadors of health. They can make their living out of selling tamales and cleaning houses. That's really impressive. I'm not an expert, but I think immigrants are making a huge difference in Baltimore.

IV.

When we decided to hire a DJ for the end of the conference, I didn't really expect people to dance. But here we were, in the small bar off the back of the venue, everyone was sweating and dancing. We had talked about everything from academia to policy, advocacy to funding. I am proud of those moments where faculty, researchers, and partners can come together to work and still have time to have fun.

Growing up, my only role model was Jennifer Lopez! I often work with teenagers through community service workshops, and I like to reach them by telling stories about myself they can connect to, such as how I took care of my siblings while my parents worked seven days each week, or how I worked three jobs to pay for school and help my parents to pay the mortgage of their first house. During some sessions, we talk about identity. I want people to see me as someone who advances. When it's time to demand, I demand quality and efficiency. Although imposter syndrome can overwhelm me as a non-white immigrant, when I meet with teenagers, I tell them I'm the boss and brag about it a little! So that they can say *that this cool person is talking to us, if she's doing that, then I can totally do it*. I want them to see that something big is possible for them.

Once, I had a meeting to advocate for more funding for Centro SOL with someone very high up at the university. This person said she didn't know what we did, and pushed me to defend the value we brought to our institution. She had many ideas for what we should be doing—things we were already doing with no money. Talking to me in a way she'd never talk to a white colleague. Finally, I said to her: I'm not a community liaison, I'm an executive director. If you want to be a part of the work that Centro SOL does, talk to me as the operator of any other nonprofit. I'm the boss. My hands were shaking and I was sweating; I felt like I had stepped up for myself for the first time in my life. Right then, I promised myself that it wouldn't be the last time.

V.

Before we leave the conference venue, I check to make sure all the lights are off, and the trash is picked up. No matter how much I look to the future, I'm always mindful of staying present, staying connected to my family and my roots. Like Jenny from the Block. I get in my car, and adjust the rearview mirror to see the pile of supplies sitting in the backseat behind me.

This conference has exemplified what this job means to me: constantly learning about the community and myself, getting creative, thinking of what we can make from what we have. All my life, I've followed my love of working with people and communities, and I feel grateful for what I have gotten to do. I don't know where life will take me in another 10 years, but tonight, as I start driving, I feel like I'm headed into the future.

# Norwood's Story – It's Common but Not Commonly Heard: Being a Tough Man in Soul and Spirit

## Norwood Johnson's Story as Told to Iraj Qureshi

One day, my son said to me, "Daddy, let's move." I looked at this cute little kid and immediately knew it was time to move to a place that was safer for the both of us. I had finally addressed my pride, which had led me into thinking that as a man, I could take the abuse for so many years. This was a moment of transformation.

Once my son and I moved out to a safer home, I felt calmer and said to myself, "Hey you know I'm in a safe place, it's all over. Now my life is gonna be alright." That is when the floodgates of all these years of keeping my abuse a secret erupted. Like a volcano spewing hot lava and ash. I had nightmares and I was depressed. I remember stepping outside on a balcony one night, it was 20 degrees Fahrenheit. I was wearing a T-shirt and shorts, indifferent to the cold, I stood there numb, and gazed and gazed for a very long time. I did not realize how long I had been standing there until my son joined me and asked, "Daddy, are you okay?" That was when I woke back up into the present, and we walked back inside to get warm.

When it happened the first time, I felt left out as a male survivor of intimate partner violence. Over 20 years ago, I met this very attractive lady. She had a bubbly personality and we fell in love. We were married and we had a son. We traveled to romantic getaways to Jamaica and St. Lucia, places with beautiful turquoise waters. My wife's sudden shift in behavior came as a shock and blindsided me.

Take it like a man, a message that was a consistent part of my upbringing. It came from my father, my culture, and from the world around me. I was a superior athlete on my sports team, and I was told to be tough and be hard. "A man don't cry," I was told. That gave way to pride, and pride is twofold. One part of it is about self-respect, but the other one is about ego which is misleading and harmful. This pride kept me from telling my mother, my friends, and family about the abuse. I could take it like a man, fix it, live it out, and keep the family together. I did that for twelve years.

One night in 2004, my wife and I had a heated conversation that turned into her hurling verbal abuse and insults at me. She continued bombarding me with curses in the morning and went as far as digging her nails into my face and scalp. This was not the first time that she had attacked me. I felt a streak of anger rising inside of me to respond back with physical force but gulped it down and called 911. The police arrived, took pictures of my bloody injuries, and arrested her. The neighbors watched as she got arrested and saw my injured face, which was embarrassing for me. In court, I accepted her apology. I wanted to keep the family together.

The abuse resurfaced, and that caused me to lose intimate feelings for her. It was a complicated feeling; I did not know if I was losing my sense of intimacy and arousal for her because of the abuse or because something was physically wrong with me. I visited a doctor who ran some tests and screened me. The doctor's feedback was the first revelation moment for me. My physical condition was healthy. The fact was that I was being abused and I did not want to have sex with my abuser. I decided to say no the next time she wanted to be intimate with me. Because of my refusal, one day, she tried to force sex on me. I called the police and she admitted to the police officer that she tried to force me into it. The police simply told her not to force me, and that we look like good people, and we should work it out. That response from the police left me feeling incredulous. If we had a flipped situation where I was the one forcing my wife for sex, I would have been arrested and the repercussions for me would have been different.

The verbal and physical abuse continued. My son would hear the commotion and get affected by it. I had already approached the House of Ruth once before. This is a non-profit that provides support and shelter to victims of intimate partner violence. I did not follow-up with them and continued with my failed attempts to keep the family together with the resolve that I could still fix it. Then my wife attacked me again one day, and this time it was not so physically violent as it was humiliating. She started spitting on me repeatedly to the point that my shirt soaked like it had been soaked in cold water. I went to the basement and sat on the loveseat in the dark for hours. I could not shake this from my spirit. I could no longer differentiate my wife from somebody on the street trying to harm me. I felt afraid of this woman.

There were several times I wanted to declare war by retaliating with physical force. I was physically stronger than her, I could take her out if I wanted to. These thoughts boiled inside of me, but as much as I was raised to be tough, I also had my Christian faith and examples of inspiring men who had never resorted to violence in the face of it. Dr. Martin Luther King was non-violent, and he exercised peace and self-control while he was abused by racist groups and the police. Jesus was abused and spat on by people, but he responded with compassion. These figures inspired me to embrace the values that make you a bigger person.

Healthy masculinity encourages men to display kindness, compassion, and love towards others and themselves. Listening to other men's experiences and validating their feelings, not being afraid to check in with friends and loved ones, seeking positive outcomes, and not feeling intimidated to express emotions freely. Men who express emotions have an increased life satisfaction and self-esteem, and decreased rates of health issues such as depression and premature death. Our society raises men to be tough and to "take it like a man" does a disservice to our health and the health of others. Without being inspired by healthy male figures, it is easy to resort to violence as a form of reaction or retaliation, especially when you are the one being attacked. I had confided about my abuse with one friend who was in the military, and he had advised me to not retaliate with physical force. He was another example of a man who was trained to physically defend and disable an attack, and there he was, telling me to hold back these thoughts that welled up inside of me every time my wife became violent.

Moving to a safer home was the end to my physical abuse, but too was the starting point for my declining mental health. A healing process was well needed. I reached out to the same friend who was serving in the military. He had just gotten back from serving in Iraq. I told him about my nightmares and stress I was going through, and he pointed out that what I was experiencing may have been Post-traumatic stress disorder (PTSD). I decided to reach out to the House of Ruth again to get counseling and help for my mental health.

My counselor would tell me to keep going, to practice techniques for managing stress and nightmares. She said I will see the light at the end of the tunnel one day. I was not seeing the light. I kept going and listening to everything she said. It was a two-year journey where I tried to heal from twelve years of verbal, emotional, and physical abuse that was accompanied with several inner battles, dark thoughts—like wanting to hit her back, and trying to maintain a sense of pride that I could keep the family together if I just kept enduring the abuse. With a healthier sense of masculinity and an incredible support system, I can now own my experiences and my journey to say that I am a proud survivor of intimate partner violence.

I was trained as a boxer, trained to disable an attack in 30 seconds or less. I was also raised to have compassion for people. I used that compassion to practice restraint. I practiced enough refrain to leave for a safer home, took care of my son and took care of myself, and with the help of House of Ruth, I have become a proud survivor.

# Glowing on the Inside and Out

## Tevis Simon's Story as told to Sahithi Madireddy

I always knew that depression was hereditary in my family. In my twenties, I did a lot of crying. I had these feelings in the pit of my stomach like butterflies, but not the good butterflies. Just that pain and discomfort, the perspiration and biting the inside of my jaw, and picking the bottom of my lip, and peeling my cuticles and biting my nails. I knew there was something going on, but I thought everyone else dealt with this too. Some mornings, I was so debilitated that I couldn't get up, which made it hard to maintain a job.

It got worse when I experienced a home invasion in 2011. The police treated me like I was making it up. By that time, I went to my doctor and was diagnosed with major depressive disorder, post-traumatic stress disorder, and generalized anxiety disorder. When I went back to work, they asked me how long this would last. It was either I resign or be fired because I was missing too much time from work. This affected my ability to maintain my home. I went to rent court to apply for a stay, and the clerk told me that I could apply if I had a medical reason. The judge got the fax from my doctor, and he said in front of an open court, "Everyone has anxiety. How would I help you if I allowed you to get a stay?"

I was humiliated. I felt like less than dirt. I honestly don't feel he would've talked to me that way if I was a White woman. I always felt as a Black woman, there are things that I simply cannot do, having a mental health condition for example. I have to conduct myself a certain way because those who know about my condition can use that against me. Even if I'm feeling bad, I can't look bad, because there's always a stereotype—that Black people, as it relates to mental health, look crazy. Or they must get high. So even when I'm not feeling myself, I always have to be on. Lipstick, hair, makeup, clothing, everything.

This sometimes discouraged me from keeping my appointments. I didn't want the doctors to see me not looking like myself, even though that's what they wanted to see. But I've learned the importance of advocating for myself after being on several medications that caused overwhelming drowsiness. I began to say, hold up, I have a right to speak for myself. I have the right to say this medication isn't good for me. Once I began to change what I wanted for me, positive opportunities began to attract to me, both personally and professionally. I have an awesome treatment team now. But that took years to get there, because for so long I felt unheard.

When I began to volunteer with the National Alliance on Mental Illness (NAMI) as a mental health advocate in 2015, I found fellowship. At that time, I was looking for education and understanding. It felt good to be in spaces with folks who also have mental health conditions. They were engaged, married, they were grandmothers, wives, and husbands. They were full-time employees, retirees, teenagers, and elders. It didn't make me feel like an alien. It felt like a tribe. There, I began to shine. I started giving presentations about my experience with mental health, which allows me to see just how far I've come. It affords me with a level of gratitude that I just wish I could bottle up. By the end of it, I'm glowing on the inside and out, because I just listened to myself talk about all that I've gone through.

I dealt with anxiety even in childhood. I remember being a little girl and doing the same thing I was doing as an adult, biting the insides of my gums, peeling around my cuticles. I was always just a sweaty little girl. And my mother was battling addiction. I spent most of my life blaming myself for my feelings, never putting together that my mom had also experienced similar feelings that caused her to self-medicate. So from the time my daughter was very young, I never devalued anything she said she was feeling. I do my best to be for her what I would have needed at that age.

But when the home invasion happened, our world was literally crumbling. I lost my job. I was inconsistent with my treatment. I had to be vulnerable with my daughter, because it was also hard for her. Imagine you're in high school, and your mom is going through things that you don't understand. As much as I was trying to act like I was okay, she could see that I wasn't. Once I began to accept that my diagnosis wasn't a death sentence, I began to be more open about my mental health with my daughter.

And I've been doing the work. I'm eating better, and taking time to get rest. The real kind of rest too, not up all night, falling asleep at 12:00 am, waking back up at 3:00 am, and then up until 6:00 am. Being around people that love me. It feels good not to have my shoulders to my ears and that constant tightness in my chest. My body feels so different now. Once I started doing all this, my daughter wanted to be around me more. She was more open to a conversation.

My therapist and doctor now, they don't make me feel like I'm overwhelming them. Throughout my life, I've been made to feel like Tevis is just too much. Like girl, you got too much going on. But I have this space where I know that I am not too much. I'm good. I'm learning to pay attention to what my body feels like, how my body responds to the spaces that I'm in and the feelings I have. I hope this inspires you to keep going. Just keep loving yourself, putting yourself first, and advocating for yourself.

# Locked In a Nightmare Cage

## Theresa (Terry) Houser's Story as Told to Eojin Choi

"Steve" was a tall, charming, well-dressed man who came in with liver cirrhosis. He wanted to use the infrared booth I had at the holistic center and learn about alternative approaches to taking care of his health, like changing his diet and trying black seed oil. After three months of working together, he overheard a conversation I had with another client about the Baltimore Orioles, so he asked me out on a date to an Orioles game—and that's how it all started. Like most relationships, we shared some wonderful moments together as he became the center of focus in our relationship.

Right before Thanksgiving in 2019, he moved in with me after his apartment building caught on fire, and we got married around Christmas time. After New Year's, he went to the doctor to get his liver checked. His liver functions were good, but his blood tests came back with evidence of cancer, and he was later diagnosed with stage 3 prostate cancer. But because of the COVID shutdown, his follow-up appointment was canceled, and he was placed on a waiting list for further treatment and surgery. He also lost his job as a chef when the restaurant closed. While my business also had to close, my clients called about home remedies to stay healthy. I switched to a virtual business, and this paid our bills, which irritated Steve.

This is when his narcissism started to emerge. His mannerisms changed, and he demanded my focus to be on him. His temper was becoming explosive. He was also paranoid and thought there were people and cars following him.

Me being in a healer mode, like a losing gambler, I was finding myself giving him one more chance to help him. I asked him about getting a therapist and later went to one of his appointments with him. I was shocked when he told his therapist that I was being deceitful and that I was trying to hide things from him. That I wasn't being understanding about his illness. His paranoia reached a feverish pitch—he was constantly pulling the blinds down and barricading doors with brooms and shovels so no one could get in.

One time, he said that people were harassing him in the parking lot. I went to the building manager and watched through the videos in that time frame. We saw Steve near his car and walking around in the parking lot, but there was nobody else there. His son gave him a real gun after this incident—I searched for it constantly but could not find it.

He also became more jealous and enraged when it came to my work. I joined him for dinner after a phone call with a male client and saw that he had duct taped a steak knife to his hand. He said that if I talked to that client ever again, he would slice my throat. He would also take my credit cards and use my phone to transfer money out of my business to his account.

Another time, he woke me up in the middle of the night and dragged me down the steps by my ankle. He threw me on the living room couch, and I could feel something snap on my back. He went to the kitchen and came back with a knife duct taped to his hand. He said, "I'm doing this so that when you bleed like a pig, at least the knife won't fall out of my hand." I blacked out and fell on the floor. When I woke up, he was kicking me on my back.

Despite these incidents, I kept trying to help him when I should have been trying to save myself. He was like Jekyll and Hyde—he was a gentle, sweet man when he was on his best behavior, but he would flip and turn into a monster. He would always grab my phone, keys, and purse so I couldn't leave.

For the first year of living with Steve, we were in a full-blown lockdown due to COVID. I felt isolated, like I had nobody. It was difficult to hold onto my sanity. My family and friends lived far away. One of my neighbors called the police after seeing him trying to toss me out the window, but he was gone when they arrived, and there weren't any physical marks on me. If there were any marks on me, he wouldn't let me leave the house. He once duct taped me to a chair and then left with my keys, phone, and wallet.

He blamed his violence on the neighborhood and the people that lived around us. We even moved because he wanted to be near his mother, but that didn't change him. If anything, moving only seemed to escalate his violence. I later discovered that he was abused by his mother growing up. When he was crying one time, she dressed him like a girl and put him out on the front porch so his friends would mock him for being a big cry baby. Another time, when he didn't eat dinner, she put him in the dog cage and fed him dog food for a week when he was only five.

When he was finally able to get prostate surgery, his pre-op tests came back positive for cocaine and fentanyl. I knew he was a recovering alcoholic, but he had never told me he was using drugs. His surgery went well, as his cancer was contained to his prostate. He didn't have to do chemotherapy or radiation. I thought that this was the end, that he would stop hurting me. But he went back to doing drugs, and the verbal and physical abuse escalated again. It wasn't until I finally got away that I also found out that he was diagnosed with paranoid schizophrenia around 4 years before we met and that he had been incarcerated for drugs.

When I could start going to appointments again towards the end of COVID, I started to see a therapist at the House of Ruth. When I came home after an appointment one day, he grabbed and twisted my arm behind me, saying, "why are you talking to people around me?" He had bugged the center where I was working because he thought that I was having affairs. In addition, I couldn't figure out why my male clientele was dropping, but they later told me that he had confronted them as they left the center.

I woke up one night with a gun to the back of my head. I instinctively pushed him away and then felt the gun. I wondered, "Oh my god, which one is it? Is it the 9mm or the BB gun?"

I was terrified, but something in me snapped at that moment. Within the terror, a spark of defiance was ignited. Years of pent-up fear morphed into anger—I grabbed a lamp and struck him as hard as I could, a desperate act that bought me precious seconds to escape. The apartment became a twisted racetrack—I kept moving with him chasing after me, shutting doors behind me to slow him down. After the third time around, I heard him go into the kitchen to look for knives. Eventually, I heard him going out the front door, so I started collecting my keys, phone, and wallet and got my dog out of his cage.

That's when I heard him come back into the house. He sat on the bed with a knife in his hand and said, "I'm gonna cut your face up so that nobody's ever gonna look at you again." But he wasn't moving while he was talking to me, which was odd. I peeked around the corner, and it looked like he was stuck, like there was something holding him there in place. His eyes were eerie and black. Then, I heard my mother's voice echoing in my ears (though she had been gone for ten years), saying, "Get out, you gotta get out now." And that's when I grabbed my belongings and the dog and ran out the door.

I got into the car before he could reach me and drove away to the House of Ruth. Fortunately, the evidence on the home camera captured 30 terrifying seconds of Steve threatening me with a gun in his hand. I was able to access this footage before he deleted it and used it to get a protective order against him. It became my shield.

During the three years I spent with him, I never knew what to expect and treaded lightly so I didn't trigger his explosive temper. The scars, both physical and emotional, run deep. While Steve's actions were likely fueled by a combination of drugs and mental illness, I know that the responsibility lies solely with him. But there is a part of me that feels maybe he was also a product of his environment and his own history of trauma and child abuse. People like him do need to be separated from their victims, but we also need to get them help if they need help, especially with mental health. I still feel that locking them up someplace and throwing away the key isn't the answer.

Now that he's away, I feel safe. I don't wish him ill but don't wish him around me either. I'm also more cautious now with people that I don't know well. It was difficult to forgive myself, but I know it wasn't my fault. What's important is that I was able to get away from that shattered life. Today, I'm piecing together the fragments of my life. The journey to healing is ongoing, but I am no longer a victim. I am a survivor.

# A Letter to My Patients

## Dr. Nayimisha Balmuri's Story as Told to Diamanta Panford-Ufere

To my past and future patients,

As your physician, I strive every day to provide you with the best possible care. However, I know that the healthcare system too often fails marginalized communities. I witness the disparities and delays in care that many of you continue to endure.

Some of you have shared heartbreaking stories that have impacted me— of being dismissed or gaslit when you raised concerns about your child's health, of suffering for months or years before finally receiving an accurate diagnosis, of having your pain and symptoms minimized because they didn't fit the "textbook" presentations we were taught in medical training.

My heart breaks for the 10-year-old Black girl finally diagnosed with lupus after months of her mother being told her rash and limp were "nothing." Simply turning on the lights revealed the classic signs that had been missed because her presentation didn't match what others had seen in training. How many more are suffering from this lack of representation in medicine?

That is why I seize any opportunity to educate the next generation of medical professionals. When I come across actual cases involving minority patients who are inadequately represented in textbooks, I ensure that every student and resident learns directly from your experiences. I insist they turn on the lights, ignore their biases, and see your real presentation. I share your stories and perspectives, so they understand the cultural context behind healthcare decisions.

Please know that I see and hear you. I am listening. Your lived experiences matter more than any medical dogma. My role is not just to treat your disease, but to understand you as a whole person—your goals, your cultural context, the circumstances impacting your health. I may not always have the solutions, but I vow to be an advocate pushing against the systemic injustices in healthcare.

I think of the 17-year-old Hispanic boy dying of cancer, handcuffed to his hospital bed as if he were a threat, rather than a scared teenager in need of compassion. How many other people of color have faced this dehumanizing treatment at their most vulnerable state?

I remember the 9-year-old girl from South America with devastating seizures whose family believed that her condition was "not meant to get better" and was a manifestation of Jesus within her body. What harms arise when we discount cultural perspectives rather than seeking to understand them without judgment?

Some days, this work can feel soul-crushing when we confront the enormity of the challenges. But then I think about you—my patients. I think about the families who persevered against all odds to get answers and appropriate care. You inspire me to continue this fight, to be better, and to hold healthcare accountable. Your resilience and hopes for positive change fuel my commitment.

We have a long road ahead, but I believe by elevating your voices and stories, we can catalyze real change. I am committed to using my platform, questioning the harmful narratives that we have inherited, and empowering you as partners in your care. Only through this approach, can we begin dismantling the disparities. I will not be a passive observer in this system, whether for those in the city of Baltimore or for the countless families who are continually subject to injustice against their rights and freedoms around the world. Your truths will serve as the momentum for transformation.

With solidarity, humility and hope,

Dr. Misha Balmuri

# SECTION II: BUILDING TRUST

# LIFE-ING IT IN COMMUNITY

## CAROL GLEN'S STORY AS TOLD TO LEILA HABIB

I was my mother's knee child, the child she thought was going to be her last. "I knew you was gon' be that special child," she always said, recalling that she wanted to name me Tametrus. I'm like, "What is a Tametrus??" When I was born, my grandmother heard carolers outside and said, "We gon' call her Carol." Carol means song of joy. I always tell my grandma she saved the day.

Being my mother's knee child, I went everywhere with her. When I was 15, my mother would take me to sign young girls up to become secretaries. I knew I was gonna get a special grilled tuna sandwich after, so I started wanting to go with her every day. At that time, women would go to stores to cash their welfare check. My mother would sit up there at that counter and ask, "Do you wanna do more with your life?" and I watched her change their lives. They would go from being a mom on social service to going to secretarial school and learning to be part of an administrative team. I remember bulks of young women who would walk in with their heads down, eyes showing they didn't see a way out. But they walked away with hope in their eyes. I wanted to be able to do that, transform people.

So I entered the health field, becoming an outreach worker at a time when Medicare waivers allowed elders to see the doctor as much as they wanted to, all with their medications and transportation fully covered. Then, the city cut the waiver. So the first job I had was to tell over 10,000 elders that the waiver was cut, and now they'd have to pay for all their visits and prescriptions.

You know, people don't care what you know until they know how much you care. Then, they'll tell you everything. I have a love for people that's truly from God, so I connected with these elders and found out many had nobody. Some said, "I don't have any kids that wanna be bothered with me. I think I'm just gonna die." Others said, "Now imma have to decide if I'm gonna eat dog food and get my medication because I can't afford both food and medications." It was terrible. I would look at them and say, "How would I want somebody to talk to my mother?" So I went between five different medical centers talking to these elders from 1996 to 2005.

In this work, I saw the way the crack epidemic tore up our city. The first thing people who were growing up in that time say to me is, "I wasn't always like this." They show me pictures. "See, I used to dress just like you," "I used to be able to wear heels like that." I look at them like, "I believe you." *I believe you.* I know what life can do to people. I know this life caught them by surprise. There was nobody in the playground when we were kids saying, "When I grow up, imma be on the street." So when I see them out on the corner, I know that's not how they thought life was going to turn out. Life happens, and you never know. One client I had was a psychologist. Her center closed because of the pandemic, and she tripped over her little dog and broke her back. She stayed in the hospital so long that by the time she got out, she had a pink slip on her door. Eviction notice. Now she's in a shelter. I call that life-ing it. One day you could be up here, and you don't ever know that you can be down here the next.

I work on the East side, where there was once this lady, Bea Gaddy. Every Thanksgiving and every Christmas, Bea Gaddy would get these huge places and feed all the poor people on the East side. It started small, and it grew and grew to the point where stores were giving Bea Gaddy free food because they knew what she was bringing to the people.

Then all of a sudden, after about fifteen years, Bea Gaddy died.

Everybody was like, "What did she die from?" Breast cancer.

Because Bea Gaddy was this little African-American woman that was so consumed with the people, she never thought about going to the doctor to take care of herself. She could've went anywhere for free because that's how much this city loved her. But by the time she went, it was too late.

Back in the 2000s, they were trying to figure out why more Caucasian women got cancer but more African-American women died from it. I hit the street and found out a lot of African-American women were taking care of their grandchildren because their children had been caught up in the crack epidemic. These grandparents became grandparents before they even reached the age of being a grandparent, so a lot of them didn't get around to feeling if they had a lump until it was too late. So I got out there and beat the ground. I went into churches, projects, and medical centers, talking with women about the seriousness of a breast exam.

I didn't think I was going to become a community health worker, but I realize that I've been ministering since I was a little girl. I started out speaking in church, and I never knew it would turn into me speaking about health. Through it all, I just hope to help people find a new lease on life, or at least a moment to smile. I love seeing people smile, so I try to get people's minds off of something for just a few minutes and make them smile, trying to live up to my name in a way, song of joy. Trust, whatever God has put you on this earth to do, it's going to be fulfilled throughout your whole life constantly. You watch.

# Where Generations Meet: My Story with Lori's Hands

## Michelle Galat's Story as Told to Bethel DeGracia

My name is Michelle Galat, and I am a graduating student at the Johns Hopkins School of Nursing. I have been involved with Lori's Hands for about a year and a half now. Through SOURCE, I found Lori's Hands, which I felt was perfectly aligned to my passion for working with older adults.

Lori's Hands is a service-learning organization for older adults in the community and helps them navigate the process of aging in place while living with a chronic illness. This organization embodies the principles of social justice by promoting dignity, independence, and social inclusion for older adults, ensuring they are not marginalized or overlooked. My value in helping older adults age in place is something that truly sits home with me. As a volunteer through Lori's Hands, I assist with practical assistance such as occasional cleanings and conversations to hold companionship with their clients. Recognizing the detrimental impact of social isolation on aging individuals, Lori's Hands creates a space to reduce this isolation and promotes a sense of belonging and community among older adults. I was inspired to work alongside the elder population as I grew up with my grandparents. Throughout my childhood, my grandparents were prominent figures who shaped my ambition to create organic friendships with each of my assigned clients. As an unmedical based non-profit organization, I have learned how to step away from the clinical scene and develop my spark for amity and kinship—morphing this aspect for my career as a nurse.

Moving from California for nursing school, it was hard not having family in Baltimore—until I encountered an especially sincere relationship within Lori's Hands with my client Mrs. BS. Since then, she not only saw me as a person to catch up with on a weekly basis, but as an important emergency contact during urgent moments, like when Mrs. BS was recently sick. I became instantly worried, so I freed up my schedule immediately to check up on Mrs. BS and provided her support by setting up two walkers around the home to provide accessibility as well as simply spending the time to chat with her. This experience highlights the imperative benefit of accessibility to resources and assistance in the home for older adults.

Overall, however, my experience with Lori's Hands can be defined by trust—not only between myself and my clients but also from hearing stories of other student volunteers with their clients. Mrs. MW, another client of Lori's Hands who is living with blindness, relies on Lori's Hands volunteers as 'readers' to assist her in sorting through mail, emails, and photos. This enables her to organize her paperwork using braille. Lori's Hands not only promotes her independence but also highlights the importance of accessible services for aging individuals living with disabilities. My admiration for Lori's Hands clients and volunteers in developing trusting relationships both in the instances of Mrs. BS and Mrs. MW in their respective situations encompasses the work of Lori's Hands.

Since moving to Baltimore a few years ago, SOURCE and Lori's Hands have helped me find a family through Mrs. BS and our organization as a whole.

# THE LINE

## ANGELA HALL'S STORY AS TOLD TO VENNELA AVULA

The line. It's where my day begins and ends at the Franciscan Center. Every morning, as I arrive, I see it forming—a testament to the diverse tapestry of lives woven together by need and hope. The faces in the line are varied, each one carrying a story that challenges the preconceived notions and judgments people often have about those seeking help.

I remember one hot summer morning when the line was particularly long. As I walked by, I saw a familiar face—"Benita."[1] She had been coming to the center for months, always with a kind word and a smile despite her hardships. Today, she looked different. Determined. "Would you like some help?" she asked. Overwhelmed and short-staffed, I welcomed her offer with gratitude. Benita, who had once been in the line for a hot meal and a bit of hope, transformed before my eyes into a beacon of assistance. She went from needing assistance to becoming an essential part of our team. She handed out flyers, brought more people in need to our services, and helped in ways that left me in awe. Her spirit of giving, despite her own struggles, exemplified the transformative power of compassion and community.

---

1. "Benita" was used in this story as a a pseudonym.

Working at the Franciscan Center, I've come to understand the deep, personal struggles behind each face in the line. Take for instance, a woman who once came to us using socks as menstrual pads. Our services were technically closed, but I couldn't turn her away. I found her some proper hygiene products, and the relief and gratitude on her face stayed with me long after. Or the man whose shoes were so worn they barely held together. Finding him a new pair brought him to tears. These moments of personal connection and tangible help are what drive me every day.

During the pandemic, our role became even more critical. As essential workers, we never shut down. Instead, we became a hub, distributing food and essentials when many other organizations closed. We pivoted to an outdoor, grab-and-go model and delivered to seniors and churches. The community rallied around us, and we adapted, ensuring that our mission continued despite the challenges. When we finally reopened, our newly renovated space felt like a fresh start—a "heaven on earth' experience, as some guests described it. Seeing people walk in, feel at home, and appreciate the new environment added a layer of joy to our work.

The Franciscan Center isn't just a place for meals and supplies; it's a cornerstone of hope and transformation. Our culinary academy, for instance, offers a 13-week course that empowers individuals with the skills and certifications they need to enter the workforce. Watching our students graduate and secure jobs is incredibly fulfilling. They come to us feeling like they've hit rock bottom and leave with the tools and confidence to build better futures.

The center's legacy is rich and deeply rooted in compassion. Founded by the Sisters of St. Francis of Assisi, who began their mission in the 1800s, the center has always been about responding to the needs of the community. Whether it was starting an orphanage or providing food and clothing during times of economic hardship, the sisters laid a foundation of service that we continue to build upon today.

For me, joining the Franciscan Center was a calling. After years in the medical field as an administrator, I felt unfulfilled. Reading the center's mission statement was a revelation. It was like a light switched on inside me. I applied for the Volunteer Coordinator position and was hired on the spot. Since then, I've moved from Volunteer Coordinator to Director of Outreach, and now, Assistant Executive Director. Each role has deepened my commitment to our mission and shown me the profound impact we have on individuals' lives.

Our journey isn't just about helping others; it's about evolving ourselves. The Franciscan Center's recent focus on social enterprise initiatives has brought in new donors and expanded our reach. This growth allows us to help more people and improve our own operations, shedding the label of "Baltimore's best-kept secret" and stepping into the light as a vital community resource.

Every day, the line reminds me of our purpose. It's a continuous cycle of giving and receiving, of transforming lives and being transformed in return. The gratitude and resilience I see in our guests inspire me to keep going. We're not just a service provider; we're a community where everyone—staff, volunteers, and guests—comes together to create a better version of themselves. Being part of the Franciscan Center is the most fulfilling journey of my life. I've seen firsthand how connecting with the right mission can change lives, including my own. It's not just about the services we provide; it's about the compassion and hope we offer, the barriers we break, and the community we build. Together, we're creating a cycle of good that ripples out, touching lives and transforming our city.

So come be a part of the change you want to see in Baltimore by volunteering or supporting the Franciscan Center. Check us out at www.fcbmore.org. Find out about our volunteer opportunities at fcbmore.givepulse.com or by emailing volunteer@fcbmore.org.

# THE MISSING PILLAR OF PUBLIC HEALTH

## DAVID FAKUNLE'S STORY AS TOLD TO MEHER KALKAT

I grew up in The National Great Blacks in Wax Museum, spending sticky summers in the back rooms, learning what it meant to truly be Black in this world—not what the world was trying to tell me it meant. The Museum was where I first became a storyteller, but my journey continued for many years after that.

I remember my sister and I being the only kids in the room at Narcotics Anonymous (NA) meetings, supporting my Aunt Val's recovery. I think back to those spaces I occupied, and I recognize that there are a lot of people who look like me who haven't been able to do the things I've done. The words loom like monoliths over my life. Black excellence. The shining example. But my mind was stuck on one word: Why? Why are we those kids? How did I become who I am when the world told me I should be on the corner using drugs? That was my first introduction to inequity. I carried the weight of that survivor's guilt for a long time. Sometimes I still do. But now, I understand why.

There are people you meet that change the trajectory of your life. When I met Dr. Debra Furr-Holden, it was like she showed me my destiny. She saw the vision of me getting my Ph.D. in public health.

I've been a storyteller since I was nine years old. I performed across the city, then the state, the Eastern seaboard, and around the U.S. At first, I was a practitioner of the African oral tradition. It wasn't until my Ph.D. that I found a new way to tell stories.

During my practicum for my Ph.D., I was placed in a substance use disorder recovery center in West Baltimore to teach clients storytelling. But when I entered that space, I found that the clients did not need to be taught storytelling—they just needed a space to tell their stories. I can say now in retrospect, that moment changed my life. It showed me for the first time that I could apply my artistic and cultural practice within public health as an equity tool. Normally in research, we look at people recovering from substance use disorder in quantifiable terms: their age, their sex, their race, their gender, their location, and their drug use. But my mind always goes to my aunt and the Saturdays I spent listening to stories at NA. There is no way you can capture the essence of who she is with data points, because she is her own beautiful story that deserves to be heard. And she showed that people would listen, over and over again.

That became my Thursday evening ritual, being in that space of healing and recovery, telling stories, listening to their stories, bringing folktales from various traditions, and using it as an opportunity to catalyze discussion. We talked about everything. We talked about society. We talked about our lives. We talked about our histories. We talked about our relationships. Within these spaces of telling our unapologetic truths, we were being healed. We. Not just the clients of this recovery space. Me too, **especially** me. Even in the ivory tower of Hopkins, I was reminded that the institution was made up of human beings. As long as a place is run by humans, there's an opportunity to connect with humans through our stories. That's what I was able to do with my professors. I wasn't presenting equations or detailed analyses. All I had were stories. And they believed them.

Soon enough, I had more than stories. I showed that we could use storytelling as a human-centered approach for qualitative data and as a health tool. Qualitative data fills in the gaps that quantitative data cannot reach. I met people who were doing this work long before me and who dedicated their scientific careers to the utilization of creative, cultural, and artistic expressions for the purpose of addressing health and well-being. And when I learned that existed, it changed everything because it started to make sense of my life prior.

I've been an artist my entire life. Whether it's storytelling, singing, dancing, acting, or even a little bit of visual arts, I am an artist. That's what I did. That's my story. And when I had the chance to think about the totality of those creative experiences, the rehearsals, the performances, the camaraderie, the friendship, and the love . . . I was happy. When I engage in arts and culture, I am happy. That's health. Happiness is health.

Through storytelling, I have learned to declare my Blackness, to make myself undeniable. When it comes to groups of people who have been historically marginalized and oppressed, I know how powerful storytelling is. It allows our truth to be heard. And when that happens, that's when equity and liberation can occur.

As a child, I wasn't told explicitly what I could or couldn't achieve, but society echoed those words around me. You can't. You shouldn't. You won't. But my village pushed back. They raised me on their own words in an even louder chorus. You can be. You should. And you will. I am a product of the faith of my people in me, and I carry that proudly. When I think of myself and my own story, I want people to know I exist. If they know I exist, then they know my story exists. And if they know my story exists, then everything else I want them to understand will be there.

What I've learned through this journey is that it doesn't matter how powerful or wealthy you are, everyone just wants to be acknowledged, appreciated, respected, understood, and loved. Storytelling, better than anything else, allows people to be reminded of that and allows them to be reconnected with their living, not just their existing. And I know that's what real health is.

# SECTION III: AGENT OF CHANGE

# Routine/Rutina

## Karen Linares Mendoza's Story as Told to Alex Kong

No matter how many times I do it, I still get the jitters. *Anything could happen.*

We never really stayed in one place for long. By the time I was nine, we had moved all over Mexico for my dad's work: from Nuevo León to Yucatán. Nowhere felt like home, but *everywhere* felt like home. We moved every year-and-a-half or so to the point where I found a strange comfort in the rhythm of the changes: *new school, new people, new culture. Adapt. Move. Start all over again.* The familiarity of *unfamiliarity* was so second-nature that when our parents told us we were moving to the United States, my sisters and I were nervous but thought we could handle it.

In the early days before school started, our dad tried hard to make sure we could integrate successfully, often writing words in English on a whiteboard he had bought for some impromptu lessons.

***Vamos hijas. Ahora tienen que aprender Inglés.***

*Okay girls, you have to learn English now.*

We didn't learn English, at least not until we went to school, but we still appreciated the effort. Still, no number of lessons or moves could have prepared us for the culture shock we experienced in those first couple months. We traded the city and suburbs for the countryside, and I saw snow for the first time in my life. Attending school was terrifying: most of the time I didn't know what was going on, but I also didn't have the *luxury* of being nervous. My younger sister and I started at the same school, which provided both comfort and a sense of responsibility to look after her. For the first two months, my sister refused to speak English, insisting that her classmates and teachers would understand her. One day, our Spanish teacher came up to me and said:

**Tienes que venir ahora. Tu hermana está llorando, y no nos dice por qué.**

*You need to come. Your little sister is crying, and she won't tell us why.*

\*\*\*

When I moved to Baltimore for college, it was *meant to be* just another new city to adjust to, but for the first time in my life, I felt truly alone. I missed my family and being able to speak in my first language when I stepped through the door to my house. While I attended college with the hopes of becoming a doctor, it was both the health component and this separation from my culture that drew me to volunteering as a Spanish advocate at the university's hospital.

For seven hours a week, I leave my own worries at the door and speak to individuals who need more than medication to live healthy lives. The need to access healthcare is what brings these clients to the hospital and our clinic in the first place, but many face challenges that contribute to and extend beyond their physical ailments. Some clients need insurance, others experience food insecurity, and still more face financial instabilities. For seven hours a week, I help to bridge the same language barrier that I had the support to overcome as a child and see the harm that it—and other barriers—can inflict.

Undocumented clients face even greater challenges: many services and jobs require beneficiaries to have social security numbers. Most are cautious and fearful, weighing their need for help against the worries that accepting it comes at the terrible price of putting themselves or their family at risk. For some, it doesn't matter how much they want or need help: they suffer so their family will not.

All I can do in these situations is reassure them that they *can* accept help without repercussions while acknowledging the fear they had to overcome to speak to me in the first place.

Our medical system teaches students to "treat the patient, not the disease," and this is a noble aspiration. But, by treating "patients" and not "people," that same system is only addressing one intermediate factor in a long series of cascading and compounding issues. I have had patients call in a panic because they received a notice that their electricity would be turned off the next day, and they take medicine which requires refrigeration. Without addressing these underlying issues, people will continue to become patients, and patients will become sicker. Healthcare professionals have a responsibility to see and help a person beyond their disease and to provide care that transcends social and economic barriers.

***

There's a phrase that my parents often repeat, almost a family mantra that my sisters and I grew up hearing:

***Para ser una persona exitosa no importa cuantos premios ganen o cuánto dinero tengan, sino lo que está adentro de ti y la persona buena que puedas ser.***

*To be a successful person, it doesn't matter how many prizes or awards you win, or the money you'll have, but rather what's inside you and the good person you can be.*

In my volunteer role, the chaos and uncertainty are constants: comfortable discomforts from the knowledge that every person I speak to faces unique challenges and circumstances. Through it all, I see echoes of my own life in the people I try to help: feelings of isolation, struggles to blend in to a new society, a fierce dedication to family, and *hope*–that there will be a time when things won't be so hard, and they can finally feel at home. It is challenging and unpredictable work, and the worries of some of my interactions with clients aren't easily left at the clinic when I clock out. Yet for the people I can help and who help me in turn to be *una persona buena*, I will gladly carry this weight. And so the routine continues:

*Enter the building. Take the elevator up to the seventh floor. As soon as you see the front desk, take the right and walk to the end of the hallway. Sit down at the small (but mighty) desk. Log in. Take a deep breath. Pick up the phone.*

No matter how many times I do it, I still get the jitters. *Anything could happen.*

# GIVING BACK: PUBLIC SERVICE WORKER, ADVOCATE, AND COMMUNITY MEMBER

## TYNICHA WHITE BRISCOE'S STORY AS TOLD TO SANDY PALUZZI

My mom was a trailblazer. She worked for the Department of Social Services for 30 years so she could help others and move her family away from the projects to a safer neighborhood and with better schools. Along the way, I developed her love of helping people and followed her into the Baltimore City Department of Human Resource, Department of Social Services. Now I feel like the torch has been passed and I myself am a trailblazer when it comes to Human resources with an emphasis on Medical Assistance and the Affordable Care Act.

The Affordable Care Act (ACA) increased the number of Marylanders who are eligible for Medicaid. When it passed back in 2013, I was hired by The Department Of Human Resources (DSS) as an ACA Policy Analyst and Trainer. In my position, I helped shape the policy and then worked hard to learn it so that I could train DSS case managers and supervisors as well as others who dealt with medicaid and medicare on a daily basis.

By helping to roll out the ACA here in MD, I became instrumental in making physical and mental health benefits and assistance available to a huge part of the community who were previously unqualified for Medicaid.

Even if all of my efforts had been classroom based, I would have made a significant difference. But I am more than that. I have been given many opportunities to directly reach out to my people.

Filling out the forms to enroll for insurance and gathering the necessary documentation can be confusing. The complexity of the application process itself can be a deterrent. When the ACA was first implemented back in 2013, my job allowed me to go to organizations, churches and community centers to help educate and sign people up for the benefits they deserve.

One morning in April of 2006, I was watching the national news and saw the cameras trained on my childhood neighborhood block. A family friend, Freddy Gray, had been arrested then later died due to police brutality. Unfortunately, police brutality is not uncommon in the Sandtown-Winchester projects where I was raised and has directly touched many of the men in my life, including my husband.

This time I was able to make a difference. As a dedicated union advocate, I helped ensure my neighbors had the resources they needed to move past the unrest.

As part of a union delegation, I physically returned to the scene to help clean up and minister to individuals where they lived. My colleagues and I set up shop at the local skate rink, churches and schools to enroll people into the Maryland Health Connection so they could get affordable medical insurance and other state benefits such as cash or food stamps. I was able to cut through the red tape and register them right then and there on my laptop.

I enjoyed working with my childhood community in crisis. If I could, I would do it everyday. I love helping others get the medical benefits they deserve and am proud I do it everyday in my job.

Since helping others is my passion, I spend free time helping friends, relatives and neighbors fill out the forms so they too are covered. Making sure people have their basic rights is an ongoing passion of mine. I am happy to work quietly for a better life for others.

Not only am I an employee and advocate for others, I also have a seat on the other side of the table. Sometimes I sit in the local waiting room without my badge completing the process for a relative's Medicaid reconsideration. At the same time, I am still wearing my DSS trainers hat. To be able to be on the inside looking out is inspiring. My position in the DHS has enabled me to gain a wealth of knowledge. While I am waiting, I am able to use my knowledge to help other clients with policies and paperwork, to hopefully make their application process as easy as possible.

I feel that working for DSS and also being a client makes me a better advocate for others. My passion shines through in every aspect of my job and life. Because they know my story, my coworkers are better able to see dignity and promise in those they serve. Because they recognize me as one of them, the people I directly help are more comfortable dealing with me. I help to smooth the process for others to receive medical insurance.

Receiving adequate health care should be a human right—it is a necessity. Whether I am reaching out to a large number of people indirectly through training or helping someone one-on-one, I am an integral part of making health care more accessible to others, a part of making their day-to-day life infinitely better, and a part of chipping away at the health disparity that exists in our country.

I am blessed.

# NAVIGATING INJUSTICE IN HEALTHCARE: A NARRATIVE OF HOPE

## ADAM L.'S STORY AS TOLD TO TROY G.

I never had the chance to meet her or her family face-to-face, but their journey and hardships have left a lasting mark on me. In June 2022, I was assigned to "Sam," a young woman in her twenties, along with her two children. They were among my first clients as a new patient advocate at a pediatric primary care clinic in Baltimore. My task was to support Sam and her family by locating resources to address their social needs.

Right from our first telephone conversation, I was struck by Sam's remarkable openness and optimism in the face of her complex circumstances. She lived in an unstable housing situation and was struggling to find a job that would allow her to continue to take care of her children. Finances were tough, and she needed energy and rental assistance. I was determined to help her navigate her situation.

However, we were hit by roadblocks from the start. Section 8 public housing had a multi-year waitlist. Eligibility for rental and energy assistance demanded imminent eviction and utility shut-off notices. She was also ineligible for the child care scholarship as it required her to receive child support from the father of her children, something she refused to ask for as he was providing them with housing.

Adding to her burden, Sam suspected that her 3-year-old son was on the autism spectrum but didn't have the resources to help him. During our weekly calls, she expressed frustration about a report to Child Protective Services (CPS), accusing Sam of non-accidental trauma.

Sam now had no medical support for her son and also felt that CPS was threatening custody of her kids. I attempted to work with an inpatient behavioral unit to admit her son, but the program had a waitlist spanning at least a couple of years.

For one of my recent college courses, I participated in a discussion about bias in the context of non-accidental trauma. Regardless of how the report occurred, the burden of this action was far too large. Sam felt the weight of judgment from those around her, and her son's behavior was scrutinized even more intensely. She struggled to find a balance between protecting her children and navigating the bureaucratic maze that now entangled them.

Despite all of these obstacles, Sam would often tell me: "this is temporary, I know my situation will get better." While her resolve inspired me, I couldn't help but feel angry: angry at how this occurred, but even more angry that Sam was forced to live at the mercy of an inherently broken system.

I called Sam every week, sometimes even twice a week, despite being unable to offer more than a set of ears. Sometimes, she would answer the call while exhausted, but insist that she still wanted to talk. She would tell me, "I like talking to you, it helps to talk about my problems." And so I listened. I listened to her talk about her extended family in Ohio and her desire to afford transportation to visit them. I learned about her dream to provide her daughter with unique educational opportunities by enrolling her in private school.

Towards the end of our time together, Sam shared with me that she had recently come to accept and love herself. She told me that she was bisexual and that she was finally starting the process of coming out to the people close to her. It was a conversation that I will remember for the rest of my life. "I feel liberated," she told me. "Things are so much better, I'm not feeling as stressed out as I used to be."

As I continue my service as a patient advocate and work towards a career in medicine, I carry Sam's story with me as a poignant reminder of resilience amidst a society entrenched in systemic inequities. I hope for a future where Sam can have the basic resources to support her kids and more—a future where the tens of thousands of families with children in Baltimore can access the opportunities they deserve. It is a future worth fighting for.

# SYRINGES AND STIGMA

## ISABEL'S STORY AS TOLD TO GRACE YI

When I was in college, my cousin died from complications of drug use. Shrouded by stigma, her death passed through our Hispanic community with hushed lips. No one talked about it. The only thing heavier than the weight of her death was the silence in our home.

My cousin's death, and the shame of the community surrounding it, triggered something in me. It is embarrassing to admit that I grew up judging people who used drugs. I only knew what I had learned in school from an outdated curriculum based on the problematic war on drugs. Afterwards, I began questioning everything I knew about drug use. I realized the reality that the consequences surrounding drug use are borne of systemic injustice that continues to perpetuate. Around that time, I was taking a class on the overdose crisis at the same time I was volunteering in Kensington, Philadelphia—a community that was grappling with these issues and left reeling.

I was frustrated with the public's response to people experiencing homelessness who also used drugs—they were constantly being filmed and exploited without their consent. I made parallels to my cousin's passing and the people I saw in Kensington. Passersby would move around them but never look them in the eyes, as if that would make the systemic, deeply-rooted problems less real. As if drug use is the result of a moral failing, despite the most commonly used drug in the United

States being alcohol—a legal substance whose users are not subjected to the same scrutiny. The legality of certain drugs is, in reality, quite arbitrary.

During one of my clinical rotations as a nursing student, I had a patient who had been admitted for an infection in his arm. I overheard the nurse I was assigned to refer to him as a "junkie," stating that he hoped we would "cut his arm off." I was disturbed by this casual cruelty and the ease to which he said it. "This isn't right," I told a fellow student. "We need to do better." I was disappointed: I was about to join a field that I revered, but in reality, still had flawed systems and providers. I also grew determined: it pushed me to educate medical professionals and students about the racist war on drugs, the history of drug use, and non-stigmatizing language.

I have dedicated myself to harm reduction, a field that centers itself around shared humanity over punitive measures. Whether in mobile units or drop-in centers throughout Spain, Philadelphia, Boston, and Baltimore, I am committed to advocating for compassionate care and policy reform. Throughout my career, I have grown to see that ignorance continues to propagate these inequities. But I believe that open discourse and acceptance will carry us forward.

As I prepare to embark on a new phase of my career in harm reduction efforts in Ireland, I carry these lessons with me. For me, harm reduction is not simply a professional objective. It is a personal commitment to ensure that no other community must suffer in silence as mine did.

# CHASING SHADOWS

## ZEV SEQUEAN MAHNKE'S STORY AS TOLD TO PREETI SHAKYA

The first time I truly felt the weight of my race while seeking healthcare was when I sought different prescriptions for my attention deficit hyperactivity disorder (ADHD). Diagnosed with ADHD as a child, the medication I was prescribed had adverse effects: it made me lose my appetite, lose emotion, and feel jittery. My heart raced almost as if it was going to beat out of my chest. When I expressed my concerns about the medication, my experience was minimized. "Everyone goes through it," she said. "Your body has to get used to the drug." But my body never did. I eventually stopped taking the medication and was left to navigate school and life on my own.

Philadelphia was where it all began. The city's vibrant culture and bustling streets were my home. However, beneath the surface of its lively neighborhoods, my childhood unfolded in a broken home. The marks it left are invisible but run deep, etching silent scars onto the canvas of my soul.

I was adopted in Philadelphia and moved to Vermont. Vermont was a stark contrast to Philly. The vibrant streets of my hometown were replaced with the serene, quiet landscapes of Burlington. The color contrast wasn't just in the scenery; it was in the faces around me and the experiences that shaped my new reality. I was Black in a sea of people who did not look like me. Philadelphia and Burlington felt like two different worlds, but it was in Baltimore that I found my calling.

When I moved to Baltimore at the age of 19, it felt like coming home in many ways. Morgan State University became my sanctuary of learning. With each lecture, each discussion, I found fragments of myself mirrored in the faces of my professors and peers. Surrounded by Black scholars and mentors, I felt a deep sense of belonging. I wasn't just another face in the crowd; I was part of a community that understood me. There, I found my footing. I earned both my Bachelor's and Master's in social work there. Studying social work there wasn't just about getting a degree; it was about understanding my roots and finding my purpose.

At 26, like many young adults in America, I aged out of my parents' health insurance. Suddenly, the safety net was gone, and the ground beneath me felt uncertain. For the first time, I was dealing with the healthcare system without assistance from caregivers. Specifically my white adopted family. They were a buffer to the barriers. Booking appointments became a nightmare—a cycle of endless rebooking and unavailable slots. The dismissive nature of healthcare professionals, coupled with the pervasive attitude of *"I know better than you about you,"* created an environment where seeking care felt daunting. The quest to find a doctor who looks like me and gets me has been nearly impossible. It's an experience many in the Black community share—we rely on word of mouth, whispers in the community about which doctors might *actually care*.

Finding a Black physician was like finding a needle in a haystack. On the rare occasions I've had a Black doctor, the difference was night and day. I felt seen, heard, and empathized with, a stark contrast to the usual indifference. It's a feeling I wish I could bottle and share with every Black patient who feels invisible in the healthcare system.

In the Black community, health is often a matter of survival, not wellness. Preventative care is overshadowed by immediate needs, and healthcare-seeking behaviors are fraught with mistrust. We've been let down too many times. I remember my grandfather being diagnosed with cancer, but he denied his second round of chemotherapy due to how it made him feel and the lack of empathetic care he received. As a Muslim, his needs were not respected during his hospitalization, including the times of day he needed to pray. This lack of cultural sensitivity and understanding is a story all too common among Black families.

Black women have it even harder. I remember one time when my ex-girlfriend was writhing in pain. The ER doctors insisted she was pregnant. She wasn't. Her appendix was about to rupture. Her heart stopped on the operating table before they finally recognized the true problem. She underwent an 11-hour surgery and narrowly survived. It's a story too common among Black women—misdiagnosed, mistreated, overlooked. The system is rigged against them in ways that are both subtle and glaringly obvious. It's like they couldn't see her pain because they couldn't see past her skin.

My experience with health care improved drastically when I transitioned to work at Johns Hopkins in 2022. The network widened; resources became more abundant. Currently, I serve as a Student and Family Engagement Manager at the United Way of Central Maryland, a role that brings me immense joy and purpose. Every day, I see the long-term impact of my efforts, and it drives me to continue advocating for those who need it most. However, amidst this transition, I find myself still grappling with the challenge of finding a primary care physician. Just as I was establishing a relationship with one, my job circumstances abruptly changed. Even with my education and decent income, navigating the system is like walking through a maze. If it's this hard for me, how is it for others? I wonder.

My story isn't unique. It's a thread in a much larger tapestry of racial injustice in healthcare. Each thread tells a story of perseverance, of navigating a system that seems designed to exclude us. We're tough, we persevere, but we shouldn't have to fight this hard for something so basic.

I work for a day when our community doesn't have to jump through hoops to receive the care we deserve, when representation in healthcare isn't a rarity but the norm. Until then, I'll keep pushing, advocating, and doing my part to make sure the next generation of kids from neighborhoods like mine have better odds than I did. My work, my purpose—it's to change this, to make sure the next generation doesn't have to tell the same story.

As they say, "The system isn't broken—it was built this way." But that doesn't mean we can't rebuild it, piece by piece, with empathy and understanding at its core.

# Discussion Reflection Questions

**Opening Dialogue[1] on This Topic in Your Community**

The beauty of storytelling is that it allows us the opportunity to dive into stories that are not our own while also finding ourselves along the way. The Facing Project aims to bring us closer together and help us develop greater empathy and community, and in the process, to best affect change. Open dialogue sessions are an excellent opportunity to widen this community by bringing others into the conversation and to continue the practice of sharing with empathy.

Open dialogue provides readers with a welcoming and thoughtful space to reflect on these stories and allows for the chance to find connection with others. It is important to note that there is a clear difference between discussion and dialogue. While in discussion we generally try to present ideas, persuade others, avoid feelings or disagreements, and solve a specific problem, dialogue on the other hand allows participants to look for shared meaning, explore differences of experience and opinion, challenge oneself and others' preconceived notions, listen and be heard, and build relationships.

---

1. Intergroup Dialogue Project. (2021, April). IDP Resource: An Introduction to Community Agreements. Intergroup Dialogue Project – Dialogue Across Difference. https://dialogue.cornell.edu/cdp-resources/cdp-resource-community-agreements/

To organize a successful dialogue session in your community, it is important to include facilitators capable of moderating and guiding the topic of conversation, creating a brave space where all participants feel heard, and recognize that they too are both teachers and learners in the space. We recommend that organizers allow registration in advance to prepare for participants, including allowing participants to disclose any accessibility needs or accommodations. Dialogue sessions should limit the number of participants to allow space for all to contribute. For a richer conversation, ensure that participants have access to a copy of the book or know where to purchase and have read it prior to attending.

To conduct a successful dialogue session, ensure that community agreements are reviewed and agreed upon by all participants. The rules below are standard; however, participants should have an opportunity to add additional community agreements to the space.

1. **Practice active and empathetic listening.** Our attention is valuable, therefore within this space, we aim to listen actively and be open to hearing varying perspectives as a foundation for an open and welcoming space.

2. **Stories stay, lessons leave.** We want to create an atmosphere for open, honest exchange where people feel comfortable being candid and vulnerable. This can be powerful; however, it depends on the trust built among each other. We take the lessons with us, however, aim to remain confidential with identifying details.

3. **Our primary commitment is to learn from each other.** We acknowledge our differences and are here to listen with open hearts and minds with the hope of creating greater understanding of one another.

4. **Challenge the idea, not the person.** If we wish to challenge something that's been said, we will challenge the idea or practice referred to, not the individual sharing this idea or practice.

5. **Be both teachers and learners.** We acknowledge that we all enter the space with different experiences and perspectives. Therefore, through the process of sharing, we can both teach and learn from each other in the process of strengthening our

community.

6. **Take space, make space.** We aim to create an equitable and inclusive space where everyone is heard and can speak. We are mindful of taking up much more space than others. We will also empower ourselves to speak up if the conversation is dominated by others.

7. **Use "I" statements.** We recognize that our experiences affect how we see the world and that one person's experience cannot speak for an entire group. We therefore own these experiences as our individual perspectives and in using "I" statements aim to be purposeful in our sharing rather than general or vague.

8. **Be present.** We recognize the need to remain physically present in the space and offer our full attention to other participants to encourage a trusting environment for honest and vulnerable dialogue.

### Guided dialogue questions

To begin the session, it is recommended to begin with an introduction followed by the establishment of the community agreements. It is encouraged to then select a story as a group and ask for a volunteer to read the selected story aloud. If time permits, you may select a second story and volunteer to be read aloud.

*Suggested questions after the stories have been read:*

- How did these stories make you feel?

- Can anyone identify with any of these stories? If so, how?

*Some suggested dialogue questions for the remainder of the session:*

- Many of the stories refer to the impact of power imbalances between various structures. When have power imbalances manifested in your life? Which side of the equation did you occupy in this imbalance and how did this make you feel or impact you?

- Often when we are faced with impossible situations, we are forced to find courage where we did not know it existed. When have you used courage and resilience to face your own challenges and do these words raise any emotions for you?

- The storytellers often faced multiple challenges at once, which greatly affected their health. Have you noticed your mental and/or physical health deteriorating when facing challenges and has that deterioration affected your ability to address these challenges?

- We are often not aware of our many identities until we are faced with various forms of injustice or discrimination due to this identity. When did you first become conscious of one of these identities and how did this experience impact you and how you view yourself in the world?

- Asking for support can be difficult when one doesn't know where support exists, or when the act of seeking support is stigmatized. In what ways have you found seeking support to be challenging and how has that impacted you?

- Sometimes the same systems designed to help us may cause us harm. Has a previously trusted entity dismissed you or caused you further harm while you were in a vulnerable place? How did it affect you and your ability to trust this entity or others in the future?

- Successful community health initiatives are built on trust though often that trust can be broken. Can you recall a time where broken trust has been partially or fully repaired in your life (at any level: individual, organizational, community etc.)? What did it take to restore this trust?

- Reflecting on moments of healing in your own life, what stands out? How have you tried to create these opportunities for others?

- Learning about each other's life experiences is an important way to understand the impacts of injustice and many stories speak of using our lived experience as fuel to affect change, big or small. What does change mean for you and how have these stories motivated you to become a change agent?

As you near the end of your session, be sure to include action plans in the dialogue. You may use the opportunity to invite participants to additional events in your community centered around the topics or issues in this book, volunteer opportunities with local nonprofit organizations such as the ones affiliated with this book, and any other ways they may get involved.

Note: These guidelines are inspired by Cornell University's Center for Dialogue & Pluralism (CDP) (formerly the Intergroup Dialogue Project).

# Acknowledgements

**Storytellers and Writers**

Thank you to all of the incredible storytellers and writers who shared their time, talent, and passion with us. The gifts of your stories are truly priceless.

**Steering Committee Members**

Angélique Black McKoy
House of Ruth Maryland

Lauren Brereton Cox
Johns Hopkins University School of Nursing

Stéphie-Anne Cassagnol Dulièpre
Johns Hopkins Bloomberg School of Public Health

Rama Imad
Hopkins Community Connection

Kristin Topel
Hopkins Community Connection

*Steering Committee also includes JHU SOURCE Team Members Who Supported the Project:*

Mindi B. Levin
Eryn Rich
R. Riel
Ezzat Shehadeh

## Resources

### Johns Hopkins University (JHU) SOURCE
The Community Engagement and Service-Learning Center serving the JHU Schools of Public Health, Nursing, and Medicine. SOURCE's mission is to engage the Johns Hopkins University health professional schools and Baltimore communities in mutually beneficial partnerships that promote health and social justice.

https://SOURCE.jhu.edu

SOURCE@jhu.edu

### House of Ruth Maryland
House of Ruth Maryland leads the fight to end violence against women and their children by confronting the attitudes, behaviors and systems that perpetuate it, and by providing victims with the services necessary to rebuild their lives safely and free of fear.

https://hruth.org/

410.889.7884 Crisis Hotline

### Hopkins Community Connection
HCC collaborates with communities to challenge systemic barriers to health equity by training a diverse workforce of individuals who champion a more just system through an innovative and patient-centered approach to addressing social determinants of health in the healthcare setting.

### Franciscan Center

The mission of the Franciscan Center is to provide emergency assistance and supportive outreach to persons who are economically disadvantaged in an effort to assist them in realizing their self-worth and dignity as people of God.

https://www.fcbmore.org/

410-467-5340

### Lori's Hands

Lori's Hands builds mutually beneficial partnerships between community members with chronic illness and college students.

https://lorishands.org/

### Centro SOL

Centro SOL mission is to promote equity in health and opportunity for Latinos by advancing clinical innovations, diversity in research, education access and exposure, and advocacy in active partnership with the Johns Hopkins Institutions and our Latino neighbors.

https://jhcentrosol.org/

centrosol@jhmi.edu

### NAMI Metropolitan Baltimore

National Alliance on Mental Illness (NAMI)

NAMI Metropolitan Baltimore improves the lives of individuals living with mental health conditions, their families, and communities through education, support, and advocacy. We envision a world where all people affected by mental illness live healthy, fulfilling lives supported by a community that cares.

https://namibaltimore.org/

info@namibaltimore.org

**The National Great Blacks in Wax Museum, Inc.**
The Museum's mission is to stimulate an interest in African American history by revealing the little-known, often neglected facts of history; use great leaders as role models for youth; improve race relations by dispelling myths of racial inferiority and superiority; support and work with community groups, schools, and other organizations to provide opportunities for youth to pursue careers in the museum industry; and promote economic development in the East North Avenue corridor.

https://www.greatblacksinwax.org/

# Sponsors

# About SOURCE

Johns Hopkins University (JHU) SOURCE is the community engagement and service-learning center for the JHU graduate health professional schools (Bloomberg School of Public Health, School of Nursing, and School of Medicine). SOURCE's mission is to engage the JHU health professional schools and Baltimore communities in mutually beneficial partnerships that promote health and social justice. Founded in 2005, SOURCE provides JHU students, faculty and staff with opportunities for hands-on, public health practice experiences with a network of over 100 partnering community-based organizations (CBOs) in Baltimore City. SOURCE responds to community-identified opportunities and has worked to integrate community involvement into the academic curriculum within the JHU health professional schools.

- Learn more at SOURCE.jhu.edu
- Follow us on social media @JHUSOURCE

# About Transform Mid-Atlantic

Transform Mid-Atlantic is a non-profit membership association of public, private, 2- and 4-year colleges and universities, including many HBCUs and minority serving institutions. Transform Mid-Atlantic provides leadership to colleges and universities in Maryland, Washington, D.C., and Delaware by advocating, supporting, and encouraging institutional participation in academic and co-curricular based public service and civic engagement programs.

Transform Mid-Atlantic strengthens the capacity of member institutions to enhance student learning and to meaningfully engage with communities, and is supported through a combination of institutional dues, federal and private grants, donations, and in-kind contributions. The Transform Mid-Atlantic office is located at Hood College in Frederick, Maryland.

- Learn more at transformmidatlantic.org

- Follow us on Instagram @transformmidatlantic and on Facebook at *TransformMidAtlantic*

# ABOUT GLICK PHILANTHROPIES

Glick Philanthropies is an Indianapolis-based family of charitable initiatives dedicated to building community and creating opportunity that empowers every person to reach their full potential.

The Glick Philanthropies family of charitable initiatives includes Glick Family Foundation, Glick Housing Foundation, the Glick Fund at Central Indiana Community Foundation (CICF), and the Glick Fund at Jewish Federation of Greater Indianapolis (JFGI). Together, we cultivate equitable communities by supporting initiatives and nonprofit organizations creating systemic change. We provide support that empowers these community-serving organizations to fill critical gaps for our neighbors.

- Learn more at glickphilanthropies.org
- Follow us on Facebook at *GlickPhilanthropies*

# ABOUT THE FACING PROJECT

The Facing Project is a 501(c)(3) nonprofit that creates a more understanding and empathetic world through stories that inspire action. The organization provides tools and a platform for everyday individuals to share their stories, connect across differences, and begin conversations using their own narratives as a guide. The Facing Project has engaged more than 7,500 volunteer storytellers, writers, and actors who have told more than 2,000 stories that have been used in grassroots movements, in schools, and in government to inform and inspire action.

In addition, stories from The Facing Project are published in books through The Facing Project Press and are regularly performed on *The Facing Project Radio Show* on NPR.

- Learn more at facingproject.com
- Follow us on Instagram @FacingProject and on Facebook at *TheFacingProject*.

www.ingramcontent.com/pod-product-compliance
Lightning Source LLC
LaVergne TN
LVHW041545070526
838199LV00046B/1832